Introduction

The old adage "practice makes perfect" can really hold true for your [child]'s [ed]ucation. The more practice and exposure your child has with concepts being ta[ught in sch]ool, the more success he or she is likely to find. For many parents, knowing how to help your children can be frustrating because the resources may not be readily available. As a parent it is also difficult to know where to focus your efforts so that the extra practice your child receives at home supports what he or she is learning in school.

This book has been designed to help parents and teachers reinforce basic skills with children. *Practice Makes Perfect* reviews basic math skills for children in grade 5. The focus is a review of math skills. While it would be impossible to include all concepts in this book that are taught in grade 5, the following basic objectives are reinforced through practice exercises. These objectives support math standards established on a district, state, or national level. (Refer to Table of Contents for specific objectives of each practice page.)

- working with time and money
- using graphs and tables
- converting various measurements
- solving algebraic equations
- working with graphs
- working with fractions
- working with integers

- working with ratios
- finding the common factors
- finding the perimeter
- finding the area
- finding the volume
- working with angles
- working the exponents

There are 36 practice pages. (*Note:* Have children show all work where computation is necessary to solve a problem. For multiple choice responses on practice pages, children can fill in the letter choice or circle the answer.) Following the practice pages are six test practices. These provide children with multiple-choice test items to help prepare them for standardized tests administered in schools. As your child completes each test, he or she can fill in the correct bubbles on the optional answer sheet provided on page 46. To correct the test pages and the practice pages in this book, use the answer key provided on pages 47 and 48.

How to Make the Most of This Book

Here are some useful ideas for optimizing the practice pages in this book:

- Set aside a specific place in your home to work on the practice pages. Keep it neat and tidy with materials on hand.
- Set up a certain time of day to work on the practice pages. This will establish consistency. Look for times in your day or week that are less hectic and more conducive to practicing skills.
- Help with instructions, if necessary. If your child is having difficulty understanding what to do or how to get started, work through the first problem with him or her.
- Review the work your child has done. This serves as reinforcement and provides further practice.
- Allow your child to use whatever writing instruments he or she prefers. For example, colored pencils can add variety and pleasure to drill work.
- Pay attention to the areas in which your child has the most difficulty. Provide extra guidance and exercises in those areas. Allowing children to use drawings and manipulatives, such as coins, tiles, game markers, or flash cards, can help them grasp difficult concepts more easily.
- Look for ways to make real-life applications to the skills being reinforced.

Practice 1

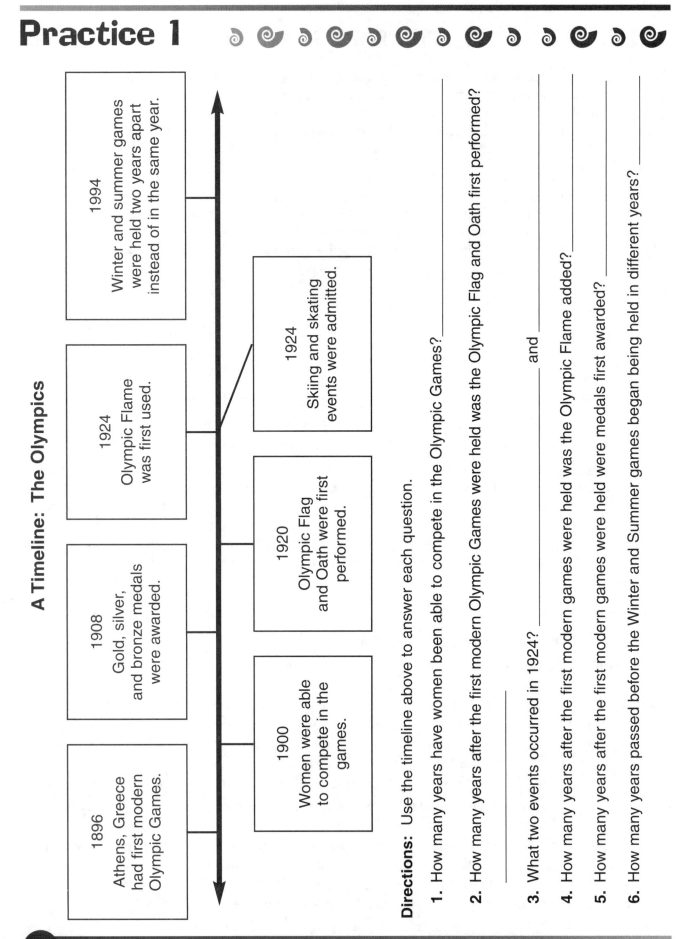

A Timeline: The Olympics

1896 Athens, Greece had first modern Olympic Games.	
1900 Women were able to compete in the games.	
1908 Gold, silver, and bronze medals were awarded.	
1920 Olympic Flag and Oath were first performed.	
1924 Olympic Flame was first used.	
1924 Skiing and skating events were admitted.	
1994 Winter and summer games were held two years apart instead of in the same year.	

Directions: Use the timeline above to answer each question.

1. How many years have women been able to compete in the Olympic Games? _____

2. How many years after the first modern Olympic Games were held was the Olympic Flag and Oath first performed? _____

3. What two events occurred in 1924? _____ and _____

4. How many years after the first modern games were held was the Olympic Flame added? _____

5. How many years after the first modern games were held were medals first awarded? _____

6. How many years passed before the Winter and Summer games began being held in different years? _____

Editor
Lorin E. Klistoff, M.A.

Managing Editor
Karen Goldfluss, M.S. Ed.

Editor-in-Chief
Sharon Coan, M.S. Ed.

Cover Artist
Barb Lorseyedi

Art Director
CJae Froshay

Art Coordinator
Kevin Barnes

Imaging
Rosa C. See

Product Manager
Phil Garcia

Publishers
Rachelle Cracchiolo, M.S. Ed.
Mary Dupuy Smith, M.S. Ed.

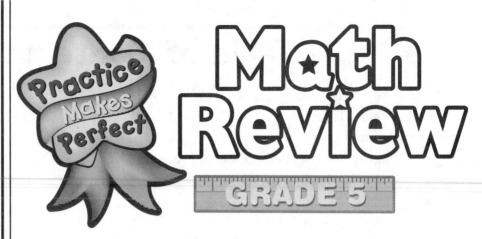

Author
Mary Rosenberg

Teacher Created Materials, Inc.
6421 Industry Way
Westminster, CA 92683
www.teachercreated.com
ISBN-0-7439-3745-7
©2003 Teacher Created Materials, Inc.
Made in U.S.A.

Table of Contents

Practice 2

Directions: Count the money for problems 1 and 2. For problems 3–6, answer the questions.

1.

$ _____

2.

$ _____

3. Jenny has the following money:

Jenny spends $99.40 buying sports equipment. How much money does Jenny have left?

Jenny has $ _____ left.

4. Blake has the following money:

Blake spends $10.38 on sheet music. How much money does Blake have left?

Blake has $ _____ left.

5. Sharon has the following money:

Sharon spends $8.68 on art supplies. How much money does Sharon have left?

Sharon has $ _____ left.

6. Nate has the following money:

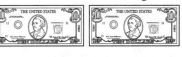

Nate spends $16.47 buying camping gear. How much money does Nate have left?

Nate has $ _____ left.

Practice 3

Directions: Find the factors for each number. Then circle the common factors for each pair of numbers.

1. **32** _____

    50 _____

2. **45** _____

    25 _____

3. **66** _____

    81 _____

4. **21** _____

    42 _____

5. **20** _____

    40 _____

6. **50** _____

    10 _____

7. **24** _____

    18 _____

8. **14** _____

    21 _____

Practice 4 ꙮ ꙮ ꙮ ꙮ ꙮ ꙮ ꙮ ꙮ ꙮ ꙮ ꙮ ꙮ ꙮ ꙮ

Directions: Read each word problem. Circle the correct operation.

1. James needs to buy a pen. The store sells 4 pens for $2.00. How much would 1 pen cost? + − X ÷	**2.** Cheryl sold 5,982 adult tickets and 3,007 child tickets. How many tickets did Cheryl sell in all? + − X ÷
3. Fletch had $85,976. He bought a new motorcycle for $18,301. How much money does Fletch have left? + − X ÷	**4.** The bakery sells donuts for $3.99 a dozen. Britney buys 8 dozen. What is the total of the donuts? + − X ÷
5. Each car pays a $1.50 to cross the bridge. The attendant in the toll both collected $13,125.00 in toll fees. How many cars crossed the bridge? + − X ÷	**6.** Vernon wants to make one and a half batches of cookie dough. The recipe calls for 1 1/4 cup of flour for one batch. How many cups of flour does Vernon need to use? + − X ÷
7. Sky has 47 jars filled with buttons. Each jar can hold 1,325 buttons. How many buttons does Sky have in all? + − X ÷	**8.** Jerry has 982 trading cards. Ben has 1,046 trading cards. How many trading cards do they have together? + − X ÷

Practice 5

Car Speeds of Indianapolis 500 Winners

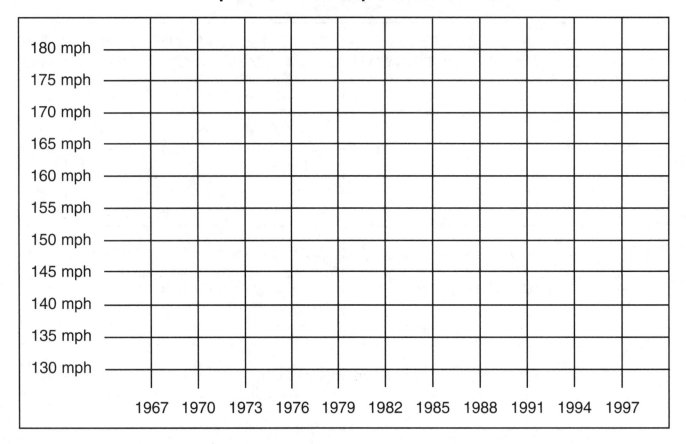

Directions: Round each winner's speed to the nearest ten miles per hour (mph). Make a line graph above showing the speeds.

Driver	Year	Speed	Rounded
1. A.J. Foyt, Jr.	1967	151.207 mph	_____
2. Gordon Johncock	1973	159.036 mph	_____
3. Gordon Johncock	1982	162.029 mph	_____
4. Arie Luyendyk	1997	145.857 mph	_____
5. Rick Mears	1979	158.899 mph	_____
6. Rick Mears	1988	144.809 mph	_____
7. Rick Mears	1991	176.457 mph	_____
8. Johnny Rutherford	1976	148.725 mph	_____
9. Danny Sullivan	1985	152.982 mph	_____
10. Al Unser	1970	155.749 mph	_____
11. Al Unser, Jr.	1994	160.872 mph	_____

Practice 6 ⟳ ⟲ ⟳ ⟲ ⟳ ⟲ ⟳ ⟲ ⟳ ⟲ ⟳ ⟳ ⟳ ⟲ ⟳ ⟲

Directions: Answer the questions using the line graph on page 8.

1. What year had the slowest winning speed?_____

2. What was the slowest winning speed? _____

3. What year had the fastest winning speed? _____

4. What was the fastest winning speed? _____

5. What was the mph difference between the slowest winning speed and the fastest winning speed? _____

6. What was Rick Mears' average winning speed? _____

7. What was Gordon Johncock's average winning speed? _____

Car Speeds of Indianapolis 500 Winners

140 mph	150 mph	160 mph	170 mph	180 mph

Directions: Make a bar graph above showing the rounded winning speeds.

8. What was the most often occurring winning speed? _____

9. Which speeds tied for the same number of wins? _____

10. Which speed was not a winning speed? _____

Practice 7

Pom Pom	Pennant	Megaphone	Hat	T-Shirt
$2.00	$1.00	$3.00	$5.00	$6.00

Tax	Shipping and Handling (S & H) on subtotal only	
10% of Subtotal	$1.00–$3.00 ⟶ Add $1.50	$6.01–$9.00 ⟶ Add $3.50
	$3.01–$6.00 ⟶ Add $2.50	More than $9.00 ⟶ Add $5.00

Directions: Find the cost of each student's purchase.

Example: Joan bought two pom poms and a hat.

Price of items:	$4.00 (2 pom poms)
	+ $5.00 (hat)
Subtotal:	$9.00
+ Tax:	$0.90
+ S & H:	+ $5.00
Grand Total:	$14.90

Joan spent $14.90.

1. Christian bought a megaphone.

Price of item: _____

Subtotal: _____

+ Tax: _____

+ S & H: _____

Grand Total: _____

Christian spent _____.

2. Justina bought one of each item.

Price of items: _____

_____

_____

_____

+ _____

Subtotal: _____

+ Tax: _____

+ S & H: _____

Grand Total: _____

Justina spent _____.

3. Frankie bought a T-shirt and a pennant.

Price of items: _____

+ _____

Subtotal: _____

+ Tax: _____

+ S & H: _____

Grand Total: _____

Frankie spent _____.

Practice 8

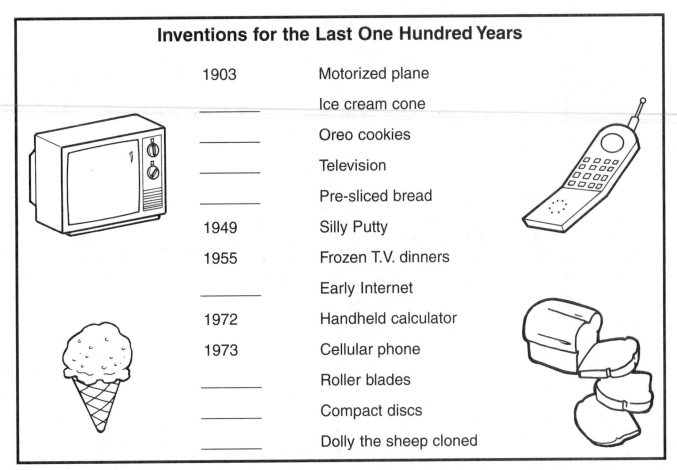

Inventions for the Last One Hundred Years

1903	Motorized plane
_____	Ice cream cone
_____	Oreo cookies
_____	Television
_____	Pre-sliced bread
1949	Silly Putty
1955	Frozen T.V. dinners
_____	Early Internet
1972	Handheld calculator
1973	Cellular phone
_____	Roller blades
_____	Compact discs
_____	Dolly the sheep cloned

Directions: Read the clues below to discover the year each item was invented. Then complete the table above.

- Dolly the sheep was cloned 90 years after the Wright Brothers flew the first motorized plane.

- Roller blades were invented 13 years before Dolly the sheep was cloned.

- Pre-sliced bread was introduced 50 years before roller blades.

- Compact discs came 51 years after pre-sliced bread.

- Oreo cookies have been around 70 years longer than compact discs.

- The Internet came along 66 years after the Wright Brothers flew their plane.

- The first television was made three years before pre-sliced bread was made.

- The Wright Brothers flew their plane one year before the first ice cream cone was made.

Practice 9 ɔ ❧ ɔ ❧ ɔ ❧ ɔ ❧ ɔ ❧ ɔ ❧ ɔ ❧ ɔ ❧

Directions: Write the time.

1. 2:08 + :06 = _____ : _____

2. 9:38 + :15 = _____ : _____

3. 3:14 + :12 = _____ : _____

4. 3:17 + :23 = _____ : _____

5. 1:10 + :47 = _____ : _____

6. 5:25 + :10 = _____ : _____

Directions: Find the length of time for each program.

7. *My Wacky Family* begins at 9:25 and is over at 10:20. How many minutes long is the show? _____ minutes	8. *Just My Dad* begins at 1:37 and is over at 2:09. How many minutes long is the show? _____ minutes
9. *My Mom Is a Car* begins at 3:45 and is over at 4:27. How many minutes long is the show? _____ minutes	10. *Stuck in a Tree* begins at 5:45 and is over at 6:24. How many minutes long is the show? _____ minutes
11. *The Tailor and the King* begins at 3:10 and ends at 4:08. How many minutes long is the show? _____ minutes	12. *Hangin' Out with My Skateboard* begins at 7:31 and is over at 8:19. How many minutes long is the show? _____ minutes

Practice 10 ⟳ ⟳ ⟳ ⟳ ⟳ ⟳ ⟳ ⟳ ⟳ ⟳ ⟳ ⟳ ⟳

Directions: Add the missing commas and/or decimal points to each number.

1. fourteen and six tenths	1 4 6
2. One dollar and forty-six cents	$ 1 4 6
3. Fourteen and six-tenths	1 4 6
4. Seventy-five dollars and forty-four cents	$ 7 5 4 4
5. Seven hundred fifty-four and four tenths	7 5 4 4
6. Seven thousand five hundred forty-four	7 5 4 4
7. Seventy-five and forty-four hundredths	7 5 4 4
8. Fifty-eight thousand, nine hundred ten	5 8 9 1 0
9. Five hundred eighty-nine dollars and ten cents	$ 5 8 9 1 0
10. Five thousand eight hundred ninety-one	5 8 9 1 0
11. Fifty-eight and nine hundred and ten thousandths	5 8 9 1 0

Practice 11 ✦ ✦ ✦ ✦ ✦ ✦ ✦ ✦ ✦ ✦ ✦ ✦ ✦ ✦ ✦

Golf Supplies			
Golf flags	$2.45	Rags	$0.82
Golf clubs	$4.84 (*per set*)	Golf Carts	$17.53
Golf balls	$0.49	Water Bottles	$0.94
Golf shoes	$3.81 (*per pair*)	Counters	$1.56
Tees	$0.01	Hats	$1.88
Gloves	$1.27 (*per pair*)	Sunscreen Bottle	$0.77

Directions: Using the chart at the top, fill out the order below to find the total cost of golfing supplies for the season.

1. 3 sets of golf flags _____ x _____ = _____

2. 8 sets of golf clubs _____ x _____ = _____

3. 10 golf balls _____ x _____ = _____

4. 7 pairs of golf shoes _____ x _____ = _____

5. 59 tees _____ x _____ = _____

6. 4 pairs of gloves _____ x _____ = _____

7. 38 rags _____ x _____ = _____

8. 2 golf carts _____ x _____ = _____

9. 23 water bottles _____ x _____ = _____

10. 7 counters _____ x _____ = _____

11. 27 hats _____ x _____ = _____

12. 11 bottles of sunscreen _____ x _____ = _____

Grand Total: _____

Practice 12 ⊚ ☙ ⊚ ☙ ⊚ ☙ ⊚ ☙ ⊚ ☙ ⊚ ☙ ⊚ ☙ ☙ ⊚ ☙ ⊚

Directions: Circle the number that matches the value.

1. ones place   2,385,131.05

2. thousands place   4,410,569.78

3. tens place   2,773,556.88

4. hundredths place   7,678,810.10

5. millions place   1,929,571.09

6. hundreds place   3,924,342.46

7. tenths place   2,299,813.19

8. hundred thousands place   8,663,454.10

9. ten thousands place   4,466,345.71

Directions: Name the value of the underlined number.

10. 4,61<u>0</u>,263.52   _____

11. 8,<u>4</u>62,493.75   _____

12. 2,277,<u>1</u>02.94   _____

13. 5,6<u>8</u>8,531.24   _____

14. 8,331,513.<u>6</u>5   _____

15. 2,866,8<u>1</u>7.81   _____

16. 7,974,91<u>5</u>.76   _____

17. 8,210,109.1<u>2</u>   _____

18. <u>9</u>,419,753.91   _____

Finding the Total Cost

Practice 13

Directions: Use the chart to find the cost of each person's SUV. Don't forget to include tax! (Tax is 10% of the total cost of the SUV.)

Models	
Basic	$16,504.00
Standard	$19,725.00
Deluxe	$21,800.00

Accessories	
Alarm	$296.00
Air Conditioning	$735.00
CD Player	$987.00
Sunroof	$1,365.00
Running Boards	$421.00
Tape Deck	$159.00
Floor Mats	$49.00

Example: James buys a Basic Model and adds air conditioning and a CD player.

Model:	$16,504.00
Accessories:	$ 735.00 (a/c)
	$ 987.00 (CD)
Subtotal:	$18,226.00
Tax:	$ 1,822.60
Grand Total:	$20,048.60

1. Julianne buys a Deluxe Model and adds running boards, sunroof, and an alarm system.

Model: _____
Accessories: _____
_____
_____
Subtotal: _____
Tax: _____
Grand Total: _____

2. Brent buys a Standard Model with air conditioning, CD player, and floor mats.

Model: _____
Accessories: _____
_____
_____
Subtotal: _____
Tax: _____
Grand Total: _____

3. Beth buys a Deluxe Model with a tape deck, running boards, and an alarm system.

Model: _____
Accessories: _____
_____
_____
Subtotal: _____
Tax: _____
Grand Total: _____

Practice 14 ⟳ ⟳ ⟳ ⟳ ⟳ ⟳ ⟳ ⟳ ⟳ ⟳ ⟳ ⟳ ⟳ ⟳

Directions: The students in Room 21 received their test papers. What was each student's percentage? Round each percentage to the nearest one.

Example: Melinda had 7 out of 10 answers correct. $7 \div 10 = .70$ Move the decimal to the right 2 places. Melinda's score was 70%.	**1.** Peter had 4 out of 7 answers correct. Peter's score was _____.
2. Jennifer had 5 out of 8 answers correct. Jennifer's score was _____.	**3.** Jack had 1 out of 6 answers correct. Jack's score was _____.
4. Adam had 5 out of 9 answers correct. Adam's score was _____.	**5.** Cori had 9 out of 10 answers correct. Cori's score was _____.
6. Bobby had 2 out of 2 answers correct. Bobby's score was _____.	**7.** Rita had 1 out of 3 answers correct. Rita's score was _____.

8. Which student had the highest percentage? _____

9. Which student had the lowest percentage? _____

Practice 15 ꙮ ꙮ ꙮ ꙮ ꙮ ꙮ ꙮ ꙮ ꙮ ꙮ

Directions: Convert each animal's size from inches to centimeters. Round each answer to the nearest tenth of a centimeter.

Conversion Chart

1 inch = 2.54 cm

Animal	Inches (")	Centimeter (cm)	Rounded
1. Common Shrew	2.5"		
2. Harvest Mouse	2.3"		
3. Kitti's Hognosed Bat	1.1"		
4. Little Brown Bat	1.6"		
5. Masked Shrew	1.8"		
6. Pygmy Glider	2.4"		
7. Pygmy Shrew	1.4"		
8. Southern Blossom Bat	2.0"		

Directions: Using the "Rounded" column in the chart above, write and solve each problem in centimeters.

9. Pygmy Shrew + Common Shrew	10. Pygmy Glider – Little Brown Bat	11. Southern Blossom Bat x Harvest Mouse
12. Southern Blossom Bat ÷ Little Brown Bat	13. Common Shrew – Kitti's Hognosed Bat	14. Masked Shrew + Pygmy Glider

Practice 16 ⟡ ⟡ ⟡ ⟡ ⟡ ⟡ ⟡ ⟡ ⟡ ⟡ ⟡ ⟡ ⟡

Directions: Use the formulas to convert each U.S. Standard measurement to its equivalent metric measurement.

```
Conversion Chart
1 foot (ft.) = .30 meters (m)
1 pound (lb.) = .45 kilograms (kg)
```

Animals	Standard Length/Height	Metric Length/Height	Standard Weight	Metric Weight
1. Ostrich	9 ft.		345 lbs.	
2. Anaconda	28 ft.		500 lbs.	
3. Blue Whale	110 ft.		418,000 lbs.	
4. Saltwater Crocodile	16 ft.		1,150 lbs.	
5. African Bush Elephant	13 ft.		16,000 lbs.	

Directions: Use the formulas to find your own metric measurements.

6. _____ (Name)	_____ ft.		_____ lbs.	

Practice 17

Directions: Convert each speed from miles per hour (mph) to kilometers per hour (kph).

Conversion Key

mph x 1.6 = kph

Animal	mph	kph
1. Black Mamba Snake	20 mph	
2. Cheetah	70 mph	
3. Domestic Cat	30 mph	
4. Dragonfly	36 mph	
5. Garden Snail	.03 mph	
6. Human Being	27.89 mph	
7. Lion	50 mph	
8. Peregrine Falcon	217 mph	
9. Sailfish	68 mph	
10. Spider	1.17 mph	
11. Turkey (flying)	55 mph	
12. Tortoise	.17 mph	

Practice 18 ⟩ ✺ ⟩ ✺ ⟩ ✺ ⟩ ✺ ⟩ ✺ ⟩ ⟩ ✺ ⟩ ✺

Directions: Convert each measurement in feet to yards and fractions of a yard.

Key
3 feet = 1 yard

---

1. Miguel cut the paper into 4-foot lengths. How many yards long was each length of paper?

   Each length was _____ yards.

2. Penny needs to buy window blinds to cover a 9-foot window. How many yards wide do the blinds need to be?

   The blinds need to be _____ yards wide.

---

3. Ceasia's bike is 3 feet long. How many yards long is Ceasia's bike?

   Ceasia's bike is _____ yard long.

4. Trinidad jumped 16 feet! How many yards did Trinidad jump?

   Trinidad jumped _____ yards.

---

5. Each wall of Bernice's tree house is 8 feet high. How many yards high is each wall?

   Each wall is _____ yards high.

6. The palm tree is 25 feet tall. How many yards tall is the palm tree?

   The palm tree is _____ yards tall.

---

7. The elephants formed a "train" 30 feet long. How many yards long was the "train"?

   The "train" was _____ yards long.

8. Garth's desk is 14 feet long. How many yards long is Garth's desk?

   Garth's desk is _____ yards long.

Practice 19 ⟳ ⟳ ⟳ ⟳ ⟳ ⟳ ⟳ ⟳ ⟳ ⟳ ⟳ ⟳ ⟳ ⟳

Directions: Find the number of inches. Round to the nearest whole number.

Key
1 yard = 36 inches

---

1. Maribella bought a chain 1/3 of a yard in length. How many inches of chain did Maribella buy?

   Maribella bought _____ inches of chain.

2. Ricky bought 3/4 of a yard of fabric. How many inches of fabric did Ricky buy?

   Ricky bought _____ inches of fabric.

---

3. Tanya cut a piece of string 4/9 of a yard in length. How many inches long was the string?

   The string was _____ inches long.

4. Buddy the dog is 5/9 of a yard in length. How many inches long is Buddy the dog?

   Buddy the dog is _____ inches long.

---

5. The cake stood 1/2 of a yard tall. How many inches tall was the cake?

   The cake was _____ inches tall.

6. Vicky grew 1/9 of a yard last year. How many inches did Vicky grow?

   Vicky grew _____ inches.

---

7. Jacob made a paper boat that was 1/4 of a yard long. How many inches was the boat?

   The boat was _____ inches long.

8. The painting measured 1/6 of a yard wide. How many inches wide was the painting?

   The painting was _____ inches wide.

Practice 20 ᕫ ᕬ ᕫ ᕬ ᕫ ᕬ ᕫ ᕬ ᕫ ᕬ ᕫ ᕬ ᕫ ᕬ

Directions: Ginger receives a $10.00-a-week allowance. The pie chart shows how Ginger spends her money.

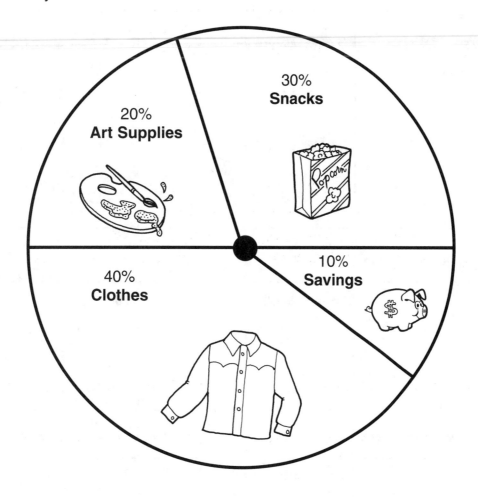

1. How much money does Ginger spend on each category of items?

   Art Supplies: _____   Snacks: _____

   Clothes: _____   Savings: _____

2. If the average month has 4 weeks, how much money does Ginger save?_____

3. If the average year has 52 weeks, how much money does Ginger spend on Art Supplies? _____

4. If Ginger uses her clothing money for a new winter coat that cost $25.00, how many weeks will it take for Ginger to have enough money to pay for it? _____

Practice 21 ⟲ ⟲ ⟲ ⟲ ⟲ ⟲ ⟲ ⟲ ⟲ ⟲ ⟲ ⟲ ⟲ ⟲

Directions: Solve each equation.

$y = 2$	$y = 5$	$y = 9$
1. $62 + y =$ _____	**5.** $47 \times y =$ _____	**9.** $y + 92 =$ _____
2. $89 - y =$ _____	**6.** $54 - y =$ _____	**10.** $83 - y =$ _____
3. $36 \div y =$ _____	**7.** $y + 37 =$ _____	**11.** $81 \div y =$ _____
4. $45 \times y =$ _____	**8.** $70 \div y =$ _____	**12.** $94 \times y =$ _____

Directions: Solve for y.

13. $y = 2 \times 6$	**16.** $3y = 63$	**19.** $y - 2 = 74$
14. $y = 17 - 14$	**17.** $y = 25 + 14$	**20.** $y + 30 = 175$
15. $2y = 38$	**18.** $y - 14 = 51$	**21.** $y - 29 = 0$

Practice 22

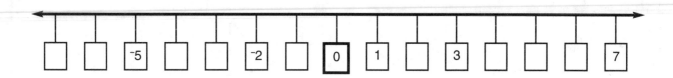

Directions: Integers are whole numbers. Integers can be positive numbers or negative numbers. Complete the number line.

| | | ‾5 | | | ‾2 | | 0 | 1 | | 3 | | | | 7 |

Directions: Add or subtract.

1. 9 + ‾2 = _____

2. ‾3 – 4 = _____

3. 4 – ‾3 = _____

4. ‾1 – 5 = _____

5. 5 + ‾3 = _____

6. ‾6 + 6 = _____

7. 4 – ‾4 = _____

8. ‾5 + 10 = _____

9. 7 + ‾1 = _____

10. ‾2 + 1 = _____

11. 2 + ‾4 = _____

12. ‾2 + 8 = _____

Directions: Add the missing sign (– or +) to make each equation true.

13. 5 – _____ 1 = 6

14. 3 – _____ 6 = 9

15. 7 – _____ 9 = 16

16. ‾10 _____ 7 = ‾17

17. 6 _____ ‾8 = ‾2

18. 9 _____ ‾9 = 0

19. 4 – _____ 3 = 7

20. ‾2 _____ 10 = 8

Practice 23

Directions: Solve each math problem. Write the letter that goes with each number on the lines at the bottom of the page to solve the secret message.

1. 8 ÷ ⁻2 = _____ **A**	2. 9 ÷ ⁻3 = _____ **E**	3. ⁻6 x 1 = _____ **G**
4. 7 x ⁻8 = _____ **I**	5. 6 ÷ ⁻3 = _____ **N**	6. 3 ÷ 1 = _____ **R**
7. 8 x ⁻9 = _____ **S**	8. ⁻3 x 8 = _____ **T**	

___ ___ ___ ___ ___ ___ ___ ___
⁻56   ⁻2   ⁻24   ⁻3   ⁻6   ⁻3   3   ⁻72

___ ___ ___
⁻4   3   ⁻3

___ ___ ___ ___ ___ ___ ___ ___ ___ ___
⁻56   ⁻2   ⁻24   ⁻3   3   ⁻3   ⁻72   ⁻24   ⁻56   ⁻2   ⁻6

Practice 24 ⤶ ⤶ ⤶ ⤶ ⤶ ⤶ ⤶ ⤶ ⤶ ⤶ ⤶ ⤶ ⤶ ⤶

Directions: Has each fractions been reduced to its simplest form? Circle "Yes" or "No."

1. 6/7	**2.** 1/2	**3.** 6/8	**4.** 3/9	**5.** 6/10	**6.** 7/9
Yes No	Yes No	Yes No	Yes No	Yes No	Yes No
7. 1/5	**8.** 2/11	**9.** 2/8	**10.** 7/11	**11.** 3/12	**12.** 4/6
Yes No	Yes No	Yes No	Yes No	Yes No	Yes No

Directions: Reduce each fraction to its simplest form.

13. 10/12	**14.** 3/9	**15.** 4/6	**16.** 8/10	**17.** 4/10	**18.** 6/9
19. 6/10	**20.** 6/8	**21.** 2/8	**22.** 8/12	**23.** 9/12	**24.** 2/12

Directions: Circle all the equivalent fractions in each row.

25. 1/2   5/9   3/6   4/8   6/11

26. 3/8   4/5   1/7   12/15   3/9

27. 5/12   8/10   1/8   2/16   3/16

Practice 25

Directions: Multiply each set of fractions. Reduce the answer to its simplest form.

1. 3/7 x 9/12 = _____	**2.** 9/10 x 2/11 = _____	**3.** 7/10 x 3/12 = _____
4. 4/12 x 2/5 = _____	**5.** 6/8 x 7/9 = _____	**6.** 2/8 x 4/6 = _____
7. 2/6 x 1/8 = _____	**8.** 8/10 x 8/11 = _____	**9.** 2/9 x 8/9 = _____
10. 6/12 x 8/12 = _____	**11.** 1/3 x 3/11 = _____	**12.** 6/9 x 3/8 = _____
13. 6/9 x 6/11 = _____	**14.** 4/5 x 3/8 = _____	**15.** 2/3 x 2/11 = _____

Practice 26 ᵔᵕᵔ ᵕᵔᵕ ᵔᵕᵔ ᵕᵔᵕ ᵔᵕᵔ ᵕᵔᵕ ᵔᵕᵔ

Directions: Solve each problem. Rewrite each improper fraction as a mixed fraction and reduce to simplest form.

1. 1/5 ÷ 7/11 = _____	**2.** 1/10 ÷ 7/11 = _____	**3.** 1/10 ÷ 2/10 = _____
4. 9/11 ÷ 2/3 = _____	**5.** 10/12 ÷ 5/11 = _____	**6.** 4/9 ÷ 1/7 = _____
7. 3/5 ÷ 5/6 = _____	**8.** 6/7 ÷ 4/7 = _____	**9.** 6/11 ÷ 7/12 = _____
10. 5/12 ÷ 4/11 = _____	**11.** 1/12 ÷ 3/9 = _____	**12.** 9/10 ÷ 1/12 = _____
13. 3/7 ÷ 9/12 = _____	**14.** 5/11 ÷ 5/10 = _____	**15.** 2/8 ÷ 1/5 = _____

Practice 27 ⟡ ⟡ ⟡ ⟡ ⟡ ⟡ ⟡ ⟡ ⟡ ⟡ ⟡ ⟡ ⟡

Directions: Rewrite each improper fraction as a mixed fraction.

1. 13/10 = _____

2. 9/7 = _____

3. 5/4 = _____

4. 20/11 = _____

5. 10/9 = _____

6. 9/8 = _____

7. 15/12 = _____

8. 5/3 = _____

9. 6/5 = _____

Directions: Rewrite each mixed fraction as an improper fraction.

10. 1 1/10 = _____

11. 1 1/11 = _____

12. 1 3/4 = _____

13. 1 5/10 = _____

14. 1 4/8 = _____

15. 2 5/7 = _____

16. 1 4/11 = _____

17. 1 1/12 = _____

18. 1 4/11 = _____

Directions: Add each set of fractions.

19. 2/3 + 5/6 = _____

20. 5/9 + 1/3 = _____

21. 4/8 + 3/8 = _____

22. 5/7 + 2/5 = _____

23. 1/3 + 1/2 = _____

24. 1/8 + 1/6 = _____

Directions: Subtract each set of fractions.

25. 4/5 − 2/3 = _____

26. 7/10 − 1/3 = _____

27. 5/6 − 1/5 = _____

28. 3/8 − 1/4 = _____

29. 5/9 − 1/6 = _____

30. 6/7 − 1/9 = _____

Practice 28 ౨ ☙ ౨ ☙ ౨ ☙ ౨ ☙ ౨ ☙ ౨ ౨ ☙ ౨ ☙

Directions: Write the ratios. The first one has been done for you.

1. Toes to foot 5 (toes) to 1 (foot) 5:1	2. Eyes to fingers	3. Feet to toes
4. Nose to ears	5. Feet to head	6. Thumbs to mouth

Directions: Write the ratios for each problem.

7. Wheels on a bike	8. Tires on a car	9. Numbers on a clock
10. Cups in a pint	11. Pennies in a dollar	12. Seasons in a year
13. Alphabet and its letters	14. Holes on a bowling ball	15. Number of combinations in a triplet
16. Stars on a flag	17. States in the Union	18. Legs on a ladybug

Practice 29 ⟳ ❧ ⟳ ❧ ⟳ ❧ ⟳ ❧ ⟳ ❧ ⟳ ❧ ⟳ ❧ ⟳

Formulas for Finding the Perimeter (P)
Triangle: $P = a + b + c$
Rectangle: $P = (2 \times a) + (2 \times b)$
Square: $P = 4 \times s$ (side)
Parallelogram: $P = (2 \times a) + (2 \times b)$
Circle: C (circumference) $= 3.14 \times d$ (diameter)
Trapezoid: $P = a + b + c + d$

Directions: Identify each shape. Find the perimeter for each shape.

1.

$d = 5$ units

Shape: _____

Perimeter: _____ units

2.

$a = 3$ units

$b = 7$ units

Shape: _____

Perimeter: _____ units

3.

$a = 4$ units

$b = 6$ units

Shape: _____

Perimeter: _____ units

4.

$s = 8$ units

Shape: _____

Perimeter: _____ units

5.

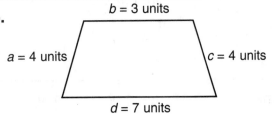

$b = 3$ units

$a = 4$ units

$c = 4$ units

$d = 7$ units

Shape: _____

Perimeter: _____ units

6.

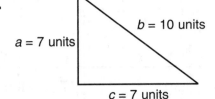

$b = 10$ units

$a = 7$ units

$c = 7$ units

Shape: _____

Perimeter: _____ units

Practice 30 ꙮ ꙮ ꙮ ꙮ ꙮ ꙮ ꙮ ꙮ ꙮ ꙮ ꙮ ꙮ

Formulas	
Triangle:	A (area) $= b \times h \div 2$
Rectangle:	$A = a \times b$
Square:	$A = s$ (side) $\times s$
Parallelogram:	$A = b$ (base) $\times h$ (height)
Trapezoid:	$A = b + d$ (depth) $\div 2 \times h$
Circle:	$A = \pi$ (3.14) $\times r$ (radius) $\times r$

Directions: Find the area (in square units) for each shape.

1.

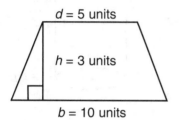

$d = 5$ units
$h = 3$ units
$b = 10$ units

A = _____ square units

2.

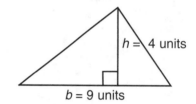

$h =$ 4 units
$b = 9$ units

A = _____ square units

3.

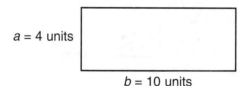

$a = 4$ units
$b = 10$ units

A = _____ square units

4.

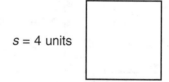

$s = 4$ units

A = _____ square units

5.

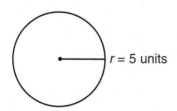

$r = 5$ units

A = _____ square units

6.

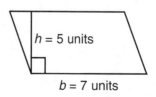

$h = 5$ units
$b = 7$ units

A = _____ square units

Practice 31 ꙮ ꙮ ꙮ ꙮ ꙮ ꙮ ꙮ ꙮ ꙮ ꙮ ꙮ ꙮ ꙮ ꙮ ꙮ

Formulas

Rectangular Solid:	V (volume) = l (length) x w (width) x h (height)
Cube:	$V = s^3$ (side³)
Cylinder:	$V = \pi$ (3.14) x r^2 (radius²) x h
Cone:	$V = 1/3$ x π x r^2 x h
Sphere:	$V = 4/3$ x π x r^3

Directions: Find the volume for each shape.

1.

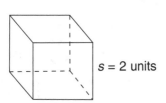

$s = 2$ units

$V =$ _____ cubic units

2.

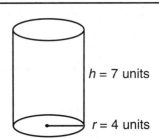

$h = 7$ units

$r = 4$ units

$V =$ _____ cubic units

3.

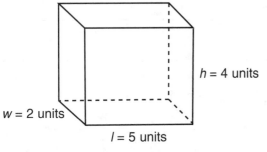

$h = 4$ units

$w = 2$ units

$l = 5$ units

$V =$ _____ cubic units

4.

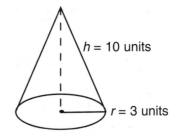

$h = 10$ units

$r = 3$ units

$V =$ _____ cubic units

5.

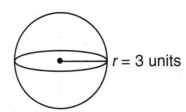

$r = 3$ units

$V =$ _____ cubic units

Practice 32 ๑ ๏ ๑ ๏ ๑ ๏ ๑ ๏ ๑ ๏ ๑ ๏ ๑ ๏ ๑ ๏

Directions: Circle the base number.

1. 2^6 **2.** 4^{10} **3.** 5^6 **4.** 9^6 **5.** 5^7 **6.** 10^8

Directions: Circle the exponent.

7. 2^5 **8.** 9^6 **9.** 5^2 **10.** 7^3 **11.** 5^{10} **12.** 9^6

Directions: Write in exponential form.

13. $10 \times 10 \times 10$	_____
14. $3 \times 3 \times 3 \times 3 \times 3 \times 3 \times 3 \times 3 \times 3 \times 3$	_____
15. 9×9	_____
16. $8 \times 8 \times 8 \times 8$	_____
17. $7 \times 7 \times 7 \times 7 \times 7$	_____
18. $4 \times 4 \times 4$	_____
19. $5 \times 5 \times 5 \times 5 \times 5 \times 5 \times 5$	_____
20. $2 \times 2 \times 2 \times 2 \times 2 \times 2 \times 2 \times 2 \times 2$	_____
21. 6×6	_____

Practice 33

Directions: Find the value.

1. $8^3 =$ _____

2. $4^4 =$ _____

3. $2^6 =$ _____

4. $3^5 =$ _____

5. $2^8 =$ _____

6. $6^4 =$ _____

7. $10^3 =$ _____

8. $9^2 =$ _____

9. $7^3 =$ _____

10. $2^7 =$ _____

11. $5^5 =$ _____

12. $10^2 =$ _____

Directions: Solve each math problem.

13. $8^2 + 4^3 =$ _____	**14.** $6^3 + 7^2 =$ _____	**15.** $5^2 - 3^2 =$ _____
16. $2^5 - 5^2 =$ _____	**17.** $10^3 - 9^3 =$ _____	**18.** $4^3 + 8^2 =$ _____

Directions: Write the missing number and its exponent.

19. $8^2 -$ _____ $= 39$	**20.** $7^2 +$ _____ $= 53$	**21.** $4^3 -$ _____ $= 0$

Practice 34 ⟳ ⟳ ⟳ ⟳ ⟳ ⟳ ⟳ ⟳ ⟳ ⟳ ⟳ ⟳

Directions: Solve each problem.

1. $6^3 \div 4 = $ _____	**2.** $9^2 \div 3 = $ _____	**3.** $(8 \times 2) \div 4^2 = $ _____
4. $(6 \times 4) \div 2^3 = $ _____	**5.** $(3^3 \times 1) \div 9 = $ _____	**6.** $5^3 \div 5^2 = $ _____
7. $(9 \times 4) \div 6^2 = $ _____	**8.** $(4^2 \times 3^2) \div 12 = $ _____	**9.** $9^2 \div 3^3 = $ _____

Practice 35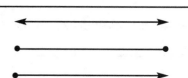

* A **line** goes on endlessly in both directions.
* A **line segment** is part of a line.
* A **ray** goes on endlessly in one direction.

Directions: Identify each line.

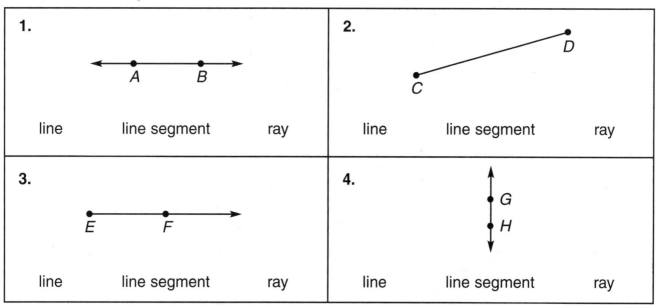

1.

A   B

line   line segment   ray

2.

D

C

line   line segment   ray

3.

E   F

line   line segment   ray

4.

G

H

line   line segment   ray

* **Parallel** lines run side by side.
* **Intersecting lines** cross each other at some point.
* **Perpendicular lines** meet and form a right angle.

Directions: Describe each pair of lines.

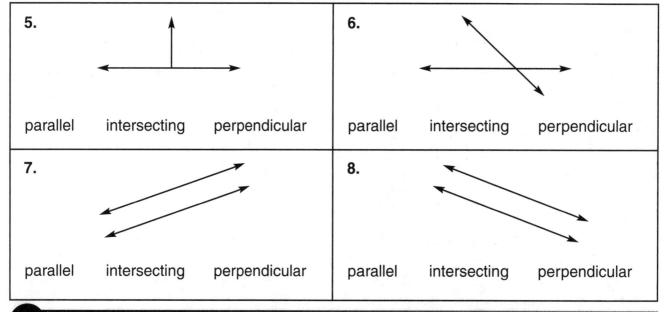

5.

parallel   intersecting   perpendicular

6.

parallel   intersecting   perpendicular

7.

parallel   intersecting   perpendicular

8.

parallel   intersecting   perpendicular

Practice 36

Directions: Write the angle for each line. Identify the angle.

1.

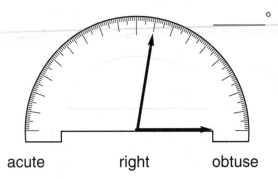

acute   right   obtuse

2.

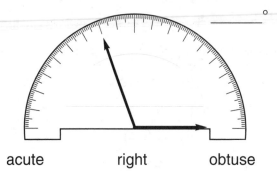

acute   right   obtuse

3.

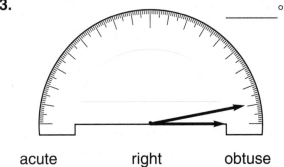

acute   right   obtuse

4.

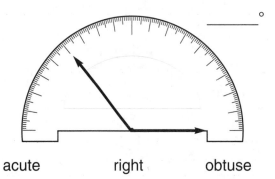

acute   right   obtuse

5.

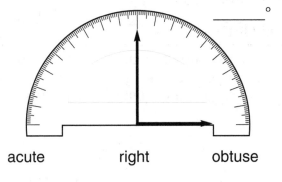

acute   right   obtuse

6.

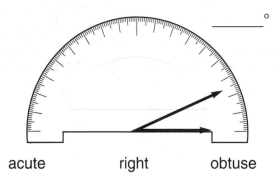

acute   right   obtuse

7.

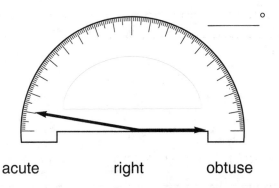

acute   right   obtuse

8.

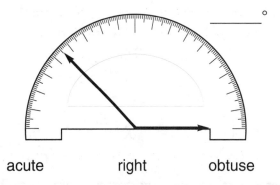

acute   right   obtuse

Test Practice 1

Directions: Fill in the correct answer circle.

Inventions	
100	Papermaking
1100	Rocket
1451	Printing Press
1620	Submarine
1765	Steam Engine
1784	Bifocals

1. What was the earliest invention?

Bifocals	Submarine	Papermaking
(A)	(B)	(C)

2. Which invention was invented more than 300 years after the printing press?

Submarine	Bifocals	Rocket
(A)	(B)	(C)

3. Count the money.

$100.57	$90.57	$80.57
(A)	(B)	(C)

4. Margaret had $71.01. She spent $63.93 buying a plane ticket. How much money does Margaret have left?

$8.07	$0.78	$7.08
(A)	(B)	(C)

5. Which set of numbers are factors for 24?

1, 3, 4	1, 2, 13	1, 5, 6
(A)	(B)	(C)

6. Choose the operation. Beau packed 10 cans of sardines. Each can held 15 sardines. How many sardines in all?

+	x	÷
(A)	(B)	(C)

7. Round to the nearest hundred.

871

900	1,000	1,100
(A)	(B)	(C)

8. Which number is written correctly?

91,04	9,104	910,4
(A)	(B)	(C)

#3745 Practice Makes Perfect: Math Review

Test Practice 2 ⊙ ❍ ⊙ ❍ ⊙ ❍ ⊙ ⊙ ⊙ ❍ ⊙ ❍

Directions: Fill in the correct answer circle.

Miles Per Gallon (mpg)	
Red car	79 miles
White car	78 miles
Yellow car	68 miles
Blue car	36 miles
Orange car	22 miles

1. What was the average mpg for the top three cars?

75 mpg	76 mpg	77 mpg
(A)	(B)	(C)

2. What was the average mpg for the bottom three cars?

41 mpg	42 mpg	43 mpg
(A)	(B)	(C)

Farm Store	
(Prices by the pound)	
Apples	$2.10
Oranges	$3.09
Pears	$1.05
Grapes	$0.94
Watermelon	$0.80

3. Bill buys 2 pounds of apples, 3 pounds of pears, and 5 pounds of grapes. How much did Bill spend?

$11.05	$11.55	$12.05
(A)	(B)	(C)

4. Beth buys a 15-pound watermelon. How much did Beth spend?

$12.00	$2.00	$22.00
(A)	(B)	(C)

5. The jet airplane was invented in 1939. The first Concorde airplane was invented 37 years later. What was the year?

1997	1967	1976
(A)	(B)	(C)

6. Abe's flight leaves at 8:27 A.M. He needs to arrive at the check-in counter an hour and a half before the flight. What time does Abe need to be at the check-in counter?

6:30	7:27	6:57
(A)	(B)	(C)

7. Which one shows fifty-six dollars and fifty-one cents?

$56.51	$565.1	$56,51
(A)	(B)	(C)

8. Which one shows three hundred ninety-six thousand, five hundred, forty-two?

39,6542	3965,42	396,542
(A)	(B)	(C)

Test Practice 3 ⟡⟡⟡⟡⟡⟡⟡⟡⟡⟡⟡⟡⟡

Directions: Fill in the correct answer circle.

At the Ballpark		Amy's Family			
Senior Citizen (Age 55+)	$8.01	Grandma	(54 years old)	Amy	(13 years old)
Adult	$13.35	Grandpa	(74 years old)	Dan	(11 years old)
Teen (13–19 years old)	$10.29	Mom	(35 years old)	Jody	(5 years old)
12 and Under	$4.22	Dad	(38 years old)	Anne	(12 years old)

1. How many teen tickets are needed?

    1   2   3
    Ⓐ   Ⓑ   Ⓒ

2. What is the total cost for the adult tickets?

  $26.70 $40.05 $53.40
    Ⓐ   Ⓑ   Ⓒ

3. Which number is in the tenths place?

746.93

    3   6   9
    Ⓐ   Ⓑ   Ⓒ

4. What is the value of the number 8?

8,543.59

  hundred   thousand   million
    Ⓐ   Ⓑ   Ⓒ

5. What is the value of the underlined number?

27̲7,610.87

  thousand   thousandths ten thousand
    Ⓐ   Ⓑ   Ⓒ

6. Joanie had 3 hits out of 7 at bats. What is Joanie's percentage?

  42.8%   .428%   4.28%
    Ⓐ   Ⓑ   Ⓒ

7. Tabitha answered 5/9 questions correctly. Tony answered 3/8 questions correctly. Who had the higher percentage?

  Tabitha   Tony
    Ⓐ   Ⓑ

8. Mushu the Pig is 18 inches long. About how many centimeters (cm) long is that?

(1" = 2.54 cm)

  45 cm   40 cm   50 cm
    Ⓐ   Ⓑ   Ⓒ

Test Practice 4

Directions: Fill in the correct answer circle.

---

1. David bought a "foot-long" hot dog but it was really only 3/4 of a foot long. How long was the hot dog?

8 inches	9 inches	10 inches
Ⓐ	Ⓑ	Ⓒ

2. 6" is what fraction of a foot?

1/3	1/2	1/4
Ⓐ	Ⓑ	Ⓒ

---

3. Derikka needs to buy 10 feet of fabric. The fabric store sells fabric by whole yards only. How many yards of fabric will Derikka need to buy?

2 yards	3 yards	4 yards
Ⓐ	Ⓑ	Ⓒ

4. Michael's turtle measures 1/6 of a yard in length. How long is Michael's turtle?

3 inches	6 inches	9 inches
Ⓐ	Ⓑ	Ⓒ

Joy receives a $5.00 allowance.

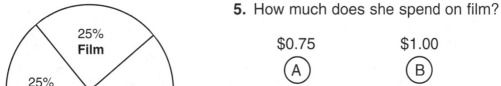

5. How much does she spend on film?

$0.75	$1.00	$1.25
Ⓐ	Ⓑ	Ⓒ

6. How much does she spend on developing?

$2.50	$3.00	$2.00
Ⓐ	Ⓑ	Ⓒ

---

7. Solve for *y*.

$$y - 85 = 32$$

$y = 107$	$y = 95$	$y = 117$
Ⓐ	Ⓑ	Ⓒ

8. Solve for *y*.

$$3y = 51$$

$y = 17$	$y = 19$	$y = 21$
Ⓐ	Ⓑ	Ⓒ

---

9. Solve. $9 + {}^-2 =$ _____

11	⁻7	7
Ⓐ	Ⓑ	Ⓒ

Test Practice 5 ꙩ ꙩ ꙩ ꙩ ꙩ ꙩ ꙩ ꙩ ꙩ ꙩ

Directions: Fill in the correct answer circle.

1. 12 ÷ ⁻6 = _____ ⁻6 2 ⁻2 Ⓐ Ⓑ Ⓒ	**2.** ⁻15 x ⁻2 = _____ ⁻30 30 ⁻17 Ⓐ Ⓑ Ⓒ
3. (3 x ⁻4) + (⁻8 ÷ ⁻2) = _____ ⁻16 ⁻12 ⁻8 Ⓐ Ⓑ Ⓒ	**4.** 2/5 + 1/4 = _____ 11/20 8/12 13/20 Ⓐ Ⓑ Ⓒ
5. 3/8 − 1/4 = _____ 1/4 1/8 1/16 Ⓐ Ⓑ Ⓒ	**6.** Identify the equivalent fractions. 3/6 1/2 2/6 1/6 3/5 5/3 Ⓐ Ⓑ Ⓒ
7. Reduce to its simplest form. **3/9** 1/9 1/3 2/3 Ⓐ Ⓑ Ⓒ	**8.** Rewrite as a mixed fraction. **9/5** 1 1/5 2 1/5 1 4/5 Ⓐ Ⓑ Ⓒ
9. Multiply and then reduce to its simplest form. **6/9 x 3/8 = _____** 1/4 3/12 3/9 Ⓐ Ⓑ Ⓒ	**10.** Divide. **1/8 ÷ 4/12 = _____** 3/8 3/12 4/96 Ⓐ Ⓑ Ⓒ

11. Rewrite as an improper fracton.

3 5/6

18/6   8/6   23/6

Ⓐ   Ⓑ   Ⓒ

Test Practice 6 ❧ ❧ ❧ ❧ ❧ ❧ ❧ ❧ ❧ ❧ ❧

1. Name the ratio.

A dog's paws to a dog's tail

    4:2   2:2   4:1
    (A)   (B)   (C)

2. Name the ratio.

Octopus to its legs

    1:8   8:1   1:4
    (A)   (B)   (C)

3. Name the shape.

parallelogram   trapezoid   rectangle
    (A)   (B)   (C)

4. Find the perimeter.

5 units   8 units

5 units

    9 units   8 units   18 units
    (A)   (B)   (C)

5. Find the area. ($A = b \times h$)

4 units

6 units

40 sq. units   12 sq. units   24 sq. units
    (A)   (B)   (C)

6. Find the volume. ($V = 1/3 \times \pi \times r^2 \times h$)

h = 8 units

r = 3 units

75.36   80.35   90.35
cu. units   cu. units   cu. units
    (A)   (B)   (C)

7. Find the value.

$$8^2 = \underline{\hspace{2cm}}$$

    10   16   64
    (A)   (B)   (C)

8. Find the value.

$$3^2 + 9^2 = \underline{\hspace{2cm}}$$

    72   81   90
    (A)   (B)   (C)

9. Write in exponential form.

$$7 \times 7 \times 7 \times 7 \times 7 \times 7 = \underline{\hspace{2cm}}$$

    7^5 7^6 7^7
    (A)   (B)   (C)

10. Measure the angle.

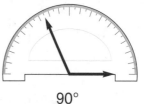

    75°   90°   115°
    (A)   (B)   (C)

Answer Sheet ❧ ◗ ❧ ◗ ❧ ◗ ❧ ◗ ❧ ◗ ❧ ◗ ❧

Test Practice 1 (Page 40)	Test Practice 2 (Page 41)	Test Practice 3 (Page 42)
1. Ⓐ Ⓑ Ⓒ	1. Ⓐ Ⓑ Ⓒ	1. Ⓐ Ⓑ Ⓒ
2. Ⓐ Ⓑ Ⓒ	2. Ⓐ Ⓑ Ⓒ	2. Ⓐ Ⓑ Ⓒ
3. Ⓐ Ⓑ Ⓒ	3. Ⓐ Ⓑ Ⓒ	3. Ⓐ Ⓑ Ⓒ
4. Ⓐ Ⓑ Ⓒ	4. Ⓐ Ⓑ Ⓒ	4. Ⓐ Ⓑ Ⓒ
5. Ⓐ Ⓑ Ⓒ	5. Ⓐ Ⓑ Ⓒ	5. Ⓐ Ⓑ Ⓒ
6. Ⓐ Ⓑ Ⓒ	6. Ⓐ Ⓑ Ⓒ	6. Ⓐ Ⓑ Ⓒ
7. Ⓐ Ⓑ Ⓒ	7. Ⓐ Ⓑ Ⓒ	7. Ⓐ Ⓑ
8. Ⓐ Ⓑ Ⓒ	8. Ⓐ Ⓑ Ⓒ	8. Ⓐ Ⓑ Ⓒ

Test Practice 4 (Page 43)	Test Practice 5 (Page 44)	Test Practice 6 (Page 45)
1. Ⓐ Ⓑ Ⓒ	1. Ⓐ Ⓑ Ⓒ	1. Ⓐ Ⓑ Ⓒ
2. Ⓐ Ⓑ Ⓒ	2. Ⓐ Ⓑ Ⓒ	2. Ⓐ Ⓑ Ⓒ
3. Ⓐ Ⓑ Ⓒ	3. Ⓐ Ⓑ Ⓒ	3. Ⓐ Ⓑ Ⓒ
4. Ⓐ Ⓑ Ⓒ	4. Ⓐ Ⓑ Ⓒ	4. Ⓐ Ⓑ Ⓒ
5. Ⓐ Ⓑ Ⓒ	5. Ⓐ Ⓑ Ⓒ	5. Ⓐ Ⓑ Ⓒ
6. Ⓐ Ⓑ Ⓒ	6. Ⓐ Ⓑ Ⓒ	6. Ⓐ Ⓑ Ⓒ
7. Ⓐ Ⓑ Ⓒ	7. Ⓐ Ⓑ Ⓒ	7. Ⓐ Ⓑ Ⓒ
8. Ⓐ Ⓑ Ⓒ	8. Ⓐ Ⓑ Ⓒ	8. Ⓐ Ⓑ Ⓒ
9. Ⓐ Ⓑ Ⓒ	9. Ⓐ Ⓑ Ⓒ	9. Ⓐ Ⓑ Ⓒ
	10. Ⓐ Ⓑ Ⓒ	10. Ⓐ Ⓑ Ⓒ
	11. Ⓐ Ⓑ Ⓒ	

Answer Key

Page 4
1. Answers will vary depending on current year.
2. 1920 − 1896 = 24 years
3. Olympic Flame first used, and skiing and skating events were admitted.
4. 1924 − 1896 = 28 years
5. 1908 − 1896 = 12 years
6. 1994 − 1896 = 98 years

Page 5
1. $99.99
2. $237.75
3. $4.60
4. $30.12
5. $71.36
6. $17.37

Page 6
1. 32–1, 2, 4, 8, 16, 32
   50–1, 2, 5, 10, 25, 50
   Circle: 1, 2
2. 45–1, 3, 5, 9, 15, 45
   25–1, 5, 25
   Circle: 1, 5
3. 66–1, 2, 3, 6, 11, 22, 33, 66
   81–1, 3, 9, 27, 81
   Circle: 1, 3
4. 21–1, 3, 7, 21
   42–1, 2, 3, 14, 21, 42
   Circle: 1, 3, 21
5. 20–1, 2, 4, 5, 10, 20
   40–1, 2, 4, 5, 8, 10, 20, 40
   Circle: 1, 2, 4, 5, 10, 20
6. 50–1, 2, 5, 10, 25, 50
   10–1, 2, 5, 10
   Circle: 1, 2, 5, 10
7. 24–1, 2, 3, 4, 6, 8, 12, 24
   18–1, 2, 3, 6, 9, 18
   Circle: 1, 2, 3, 6
8. 14–1, 2, 7, 14
   21–1, 3, 7, 21
   Circle: 1, 7

Page 7
1. ÷
2. +
3. −
4. x
5. ÷
6. x
7. x
8. +

Page 8
1. 150
2. 160
3. 160
4. 150
5. 160
6. 140
7. 180
8. 150
9. 150
10. 160
11. 160

Page 9
*(using the rounded numbers)
1. 1988
2. 140 mph
3. 1991
4. 180 mph
5. 180 − 140 = 40 mph
6. 160 + 140 + 180 = 480 ÷ 3 = 160 mph
7. 160 + 160 = 320 ÷ 2 = 160 mph
8. 160 mph
9. 140 mph, 180 mph
10. 170 mph

Page 10
1. $3.00
   Subtotal: $3.00
   Tax: $0.30
   S & H: $1.50
   Grand Total: $4.80
   Christian spent $4.80.
2. $2.00
   $1.00
   $3.00
   $5.00
   + $6.00
   Subtotal: $17.00
   Tax: $1.70
   S & H: $5.00
   Grand Total: $23.70
   Justina spent $23.70.
3. $6.00
   + $1.00
   Subtotal: $7.00
   Tax: $0.70
   S & H: $3.50
   Grand Total: $11.20
   Frankie spent $11.20.

Page 11
1904 Ice cream cone
1911 Oreo cookies
1927 Television
1930 Pre-sliced bread
1969 Early Internet
1980 Roller blades
1981 Compact discs
1993 Dolly the sheep cloned

Page 12
1. 2:14
2. 9:53
3. 3:26
4. 3:40
5. 1:57
6. 5:35
7. 55 minutes
8. 32 minutes
9. 42 minutes
10. 39 minutes
11. 58 minutes
12. 48 minutes

Page 13
1. 14.6
2. $1.46
3. 14.6
4. $75.44
5. 754.4
6. 7,544
7. 75.44
8. 58,910
9. $589.10
10. 5,891.0
11. 58.910

Page 14
1. 3 x $2.45 = $7.35
2. 8 x $4.84 = $38.72
3. 10 x $0.49 = $4.90
4. 7 x $3.81 = $26.67
5. 59 x $0.01 = $0.59
6. 4 x $1.27 = $5.08
7. 38 x $0.82 = $31.16
8. 2 x $17.53 = $35.06
9. 23 x $0.94 = $21.62
10. 7 x $1.56 = $10.92
11. 27 x $1.88 = $50.76
12. 11 x $0.77 = $8.47
Grand Total: $241.30

Page 15
1. 1 (3rd number from the right)
2. 0
3. 5 (4th number from the right)
4. 0 (1st number on the right)
5. 1 (1st number on the left)
6. 3 (5th number from the right)
7. 1 (2nd number from the right)
8. 6 (2nd number from the left)
9. 6 (3rd number from the left)
10. thousands
11. hundred thousands
12. hundreds
13. ten thousands
14. tenths
15. tens
16. ones
17. hundredths
18. millions

Page 16
1. $21,800.00
   $421.00
   $1,365.00
   $296.00
   Subtotal: $23,882.00
   Tax: $2,388.20
   Grand Total: $26,270.20
2. $19,725.00
   $735.00
   $987.00
   $49.00
   Subtotal: $21,496.00
   Tax: $2,149.60
   Grand Total: $23,645.60
3. $21,800.00
   $159.00
   $421.00
   $296.00
   Subtotal: $22,676.00
   Tax: $2,267.60
   Grand Total: $24,943.60

Page 17
1. 57%
2. 63%
3. 17%
4. 56%
5. 90%
6. 100%
7. 33%
8. Bobby
9. Jack

Page 18
1. 6.35, 6.4
2. 5.842, 5.8
3. 2.794, 2.8
4. 4.064, 4.1
5. 4.572, 4.6
6. 6.096, 6.1
7. 3.556, 3.6
8. 5.08, 5.1
9. 10.00 cm
10. 2.0 cm
11. 29.58 cm
12. 1.24 cm
13. 3.6 cm
14. 10.7 cm

Page 19
1. 2.7 m, 155.25 kg
2. 8.4 m, 225 kg
3. 33 m, 188,100 kg
4. 4.8 m, 517.5 kg
5. 3.9 m, 7,200 kg
6. Answers will vary.

Page 20
1. 32 kph
2. 112 kph
3. 48 kph
4. 57.6 kph
5. .048 kph
6. 44.624 kph
7. 80 kph
8. 347.2 kph
9. 108.8 kph
10. 1.872 kph
11. 88 kph
12. .272 kph

Page 21
1. 1 1/3
2. 3
3. 1
4. 5 1/3
5. 2 2/3
6. 8 1/3
7. 10
8. 4 2/3

Page 22
1. 12   5. 18
2. 27   6. 4
3. 16   7. 9
4. 20   8. 6

Page 23
1. Art Supplies: $2.00
   Snacks: $3.00
   Clothes: $4.00
   Savings: $1.00
2. $4.00
3. $2.00 x 52 = $104.00
4. 7 weeks

Page 24
1. 64   12. 846
2. 87   13. 12
3. 18   14. 3
4. 90   15. 19
5. 235   16. 21
6. 49   17. 39
7. 42   18. 65
8. 14   19. 76
9. 101   20. 145
10. 74   21. 29
11. 9

Page 25
Number line: ⁻7, ⁻6, (⁻5), ⁻4, ⁻3, (⁻2), ⁻1, (0), (1), 2, (3), 4, 5, 6, (7)
1. 7   11. ⁻2
2. ⁻7   12. 6
3. 7   13. ⁻
4. ⁻6   14. ⁻
5. 2   15. ⁻
6. 0   16. ⁻
7. 8   17. +
8. 5   18. +
9. 6   19. ⁻
10. ⁻1   20. +

Page 26
1. ⁻4   5. ⁻2
2. ⁻3   6. 3
3. ⁻6   7. ⁻72
4. ⁻56   8. ⁻24
Message: Integers are interesting.

Page 27
1. yes
2. yes
3. no
4. no
5. no
6. yes
7. yes
8. yes
9. no
10. yes
11. no
12. no
13. 5/6
14. 1/3
15. 2/3
16. 4/5
17. 2/5
18. 2/3
19. 3/5
20. 3/4
21. 1/4
22. 2/3
23. 3/4
24. 1/6
25. 1/2, 3/6, 4/8
26. 4/5, 12/15
27. 1/8, 2/16

Page 28
1. 9/28
2. 9/55
3. 7/40
4. 2/15
5. 7/12
6. 1/6
7. 1/24
8. 32/55
9. 16/81
10. 1/3
11. 1/11
12. 1/4
13. 4/11
14. 3/10
15. 4/33

Page 29
1. 11/35
2. 11/70
3. 1/2
4. 1 5/22
5. 1 5/6
6. 3 1/9
7. 18/25
8. 1 1/2
9. 72/77
10. 1 7/48

11. 1/4
12. 10 4/5
13. 4/7
14. 10/11
15. 1 1/4

Page 30
1. 1 3/10
2. 1 2/7
3. 1 1/4
4. 1 9/11
5. 1 1/9
6. 1 1/8
7. 1 1/4
8. 1 2/3
9. 1 1/5
10. 11/10
11. 12/11
12. 7/4
13. 15/10
14. 12/8
15. 19/7
16. 15/11
17. 13/12
18. 15/11
19. 9/6 or 1 1/2
20. 8/9
21. 7/8
22. 39/35 or 1 4/35
23. 5/6
24. 7/24
25. 2/15
26. 11/30
27. 19/30
28. 1/8
29. 7/18
30. 47/63

Page 31
1. 5:1   10. 2:1
2. 2:10   11. 100:1
3. 2:10   12. 4:1
4. 1:2   13. 1:26
5. 2:1   14. 3:1
6. 2:1   15. 3:1
7. 2:1   16. 50:1
8. 4:1   17. 50:1
9. 12:1   18. 6:1

Page 32
1. Circle, 15.7
2. Parallelogram, 20
3. Rectangle, 20
4. Square, 32

5. Trapezoid, 18
6. Triangle, 24

Page 33
1. 22.5
2. 18
3. 40
4. 16
5. 78.5
6. 35

Page 34
1. 8
2. 351.68
3. 40
4. 94.2
5. 113.04

Page 35
1. 2   12. 6
2. 4   13. 10³
3. 5   14. 3¹⁰
4. 9   15. 9²
5. 5   16. 8⁴
6. 10   17. 7⁵
7. 5   18. 4³
8. 6   19. 5⁷
9. 2   20. 2⁹
10. 3   21. 6²
11. 10

Page 36
1. 512   12. 100
2. 256   13. 128
3. 64   14. 265
4. 243   15. 16
5. 256   16. 7
6. 1,296   17. 271
7. 1,000   18. 128
8. 81   19. 5²
9. 343   20. 2²
10. 128   21. 8²
11. 3,125

Page 37
1. 54   6. 5
2. 27   7. 1
3. 1   8. 12
4. 3   9. 3
5. 3

Page 38
1. line
2. line segment
3. ray
4. line

5. perpendicular
6. intersecting
7. parallel
8. parallel

Page 39
1. 80°, acute
2. 110°, obtuse
3. 10°, acute
4. 130°, obtuse
5. 90°, right
6. 25°, acute
7. 170°, obtuse
8. 135°, obtuse

Page 40
1. C
2. B
3. B
4. C
5. A
6. B
7. A
8. B

Page 41
1. A   5. C
2. B   6. C
3. C   7. A
4. A   8. C

Page 42
1. A   5. C
2. B   6. A
3. C   7. A
4. B   8. A

Page 43
1. B   6. A
2. B   7. C
3. C   8. A
4. B   9. C
5. C

Page 44
1. C   7. B
2. B   8. C
3. C   9. A
4. C   10. A
5. B   11. C
6. A

Page 45
1. C   5. C   8. C
2. A   6. A   9. B
3. B   7. C   10. C
4. C